# In the Time of Noah

N.D. Wilson
*illustrated by Peter Bentley*

THE OLD STORIES
canonpress
*Moscow, Idaho*

THE OLD STORIES

# The Dragon and the Garden
# In the Time of Noah
# The Sword of Abram

N.D. Wilson, *In the Time of Noah*
Text copyright © 2007 by N. D. Wilson
Illustrations copyright © 2007 by Peter Bentley

Published by Canon Press
P.O. Box 8729, Moscow, ID  83843
800-488-2034 | www.canonpress.com

Cover design by Laura Blakey.
Cover illustrations © 2007 by Peter Bentley.
Printed in the United States of America.

*In the Time of Noah* uses the version of the Deluge story told by many church fathers from the first several centuries after Christ. Nemesius of Emesa, Ambrose, and Clement of Alexandria are just a few. Augustine believed the giants were true giants, but were not the descendants of angelic beings. Others deny both elements of the story and, of course, today it's not difficult to find theologians who deny the story in its entirety.

*Library of Congress Cataloging-in-Publication Data*
Wilson, N. D.
  In the time of Noah / N.D. Wilson; illustrated by Peter Bentley.
    p. cm. -- (The old stories ; #2)
  ISBN-13: 978-1-59128-045-3 (hardcover)
  ISBN-10: 1-59128-045-1 (hardcover)
  1. Noah (Biblical figure)--Juvenile literature.  I. Bentley, Peter V., ill. II. Title. III. Series.
  BS580.N6W55 2007
  222'.1109505--dc22
                                                        2007008555

13 14 15 16 17 18 19        10 9 8 7 6 5 4 3 2

For my grandfather,
who is an ent.
NDW


For Roseann
PB

While the world was still young, men and women went out into the wilds and built cities. They labored hard and grew weary because the ground had been cursed by God and would not give them food easily.

The Dragon had lied to man in the Garden, and now the Dragon's servants desired power over all of the fallen world.

The Dragon had been a son of God in Heaven—even governing his own stars. But he had rebelled and disobeyed, and the Maker cast him down from the sky along with one third of the heavenly sons and angels who had rebelled with him.

On Earth, they saw men building their cities, and they saw that the daughters of men were beautiful.

They married beautiful women and had sons. Enormous sons. Sons with flesh like Adam but strength like their fathers. These boys each had six toes on their feet and six fingers on each hand. And when they grew, they were mighty—men of renown. No son of Adam could stand and fight one of these creatures. They were giants and they were called the Nephilim.

Throughout all the Earth, these giants ruled the cities and took women to be their wives. And the sons and daughters of Adam and Eve looked to them and worshipped them.

"We have been thrown out of paradise," they said. "But these god-men, the Nephilim, will make the world whole again."

But the god-men were evil, destroyers. They served themselves and their fathers—the servants of the Dragon.

One man, Noah, remembered the Maker of the world. He and his family served God in Heaven and not the great six-fingered creatures on earth. They did not offer fruit and meat to the idols, and they kept themselves from the dark cities.

Because of this, God in Heaven spoke to Noah.

"I wish I had not made this Earth," He said, "or man, who has forgotten Me. Man's wickedness is now great, and every thought in his mind is evil. He is a destroyer, dreaming of nothing but power and bloodshed.

"I will unmake this world and man with it. I will shatter these creatures he worships with darkness and blood, and all the beasts on the Earth with them. I will wipe this world clean because of the violence in the heart of all men. But you Noah, you and your family, will live.

"Build for Me a great boat."

For one hundred and twenty years Noah worked as the world's Maker told him. He built an enormous boat, as long as four hundred and fifty of his feet, seventy-five wide, and forty-five tall. He built three decks and coated the inside and outside with the sap of trees.

Then he went out to tame the animals.

The sons of Adam and the mighty men all laughed at Noah with his great boat, sitting on the land. They laughed while he tamed animals and brought them into the pens he had built inside.

Of every animal that was clean to eat, he brought seven onto his boat. Of every animal that was unclean he brought two.

He brought in the broad-chested cats from the plains and the huge-bodied river horses. He called down the phoenix from the cliffs and tamed winged serpents that basked on the hot rocks in the desert at night.

Of the great creatures—behemoth, leviathan, and the huge scaled kings of the wild—he gathered young ones from nests and dens and the hidden places beside cool rivers.

Noah and his sons did this. They tamed and handled creatures who had obeyed no man since Adam, and Noah reminded them of the names they had been given in the lost Garden.

Noah was six hundred years old when the rains came. On the day he took his wife and his three sons and their wives into the boat, God struck the Earth and it shook. Great fountains from below burst open and spewed water and fire and slow-crawling rock upon the world. Rain and wind came from above.

The world drowned for forty days and forty nights, until every man and woman and animal that moved on the land had died.

Only Noah and those in the boat lived.

The world was silent in its grave for one hundred and fifty days. The rain stopped and hot breezes stirred the ash on the swollen water while forests floated on their sides.

The only life, the only snorting and stamping and braying and breathing, came from the great boat where Noah stood and waited for the waters to recede and for the mountains, freshly splintered from the world's bones, to stand dry.

One mountain did, and it was called Ararat. While the water still lapped, Noah's boat rested on its slopes.

Noah waited long in his boat on the mountain before he opened a window and sent out a raven and a dove, to see if the land was dry. But the birds found no rest.

He waited another seven days and sent the dove to fly again, and this time the bird returned gripping an olive leaf.

Noah waited another week, and when he sent out the dove again, it flew far and did not return.

Then Noah threw open the doors of the ark and stepped out into the baptized world, and the ground beneath his feet was dry.

He obeyed the world's Maker and brought out every beast and creature he had penned within his boat: the birds and cattle, the creeping things and the fast-growing beasts who would rule the wilds. He sent them out into world in their pairs, and they obeyed his voice, searching for dens and caves, for places to nest and raise their young to fill the world.

In the vast uncrowded world, Noah and his family thanked their Lord for sparing them. They built an altar and offered prayers to God, and He heard them and smelled their sacrifice.

Then the Lord and Maker swore an oath. Though man's heart was evil, the Lord swore that He would turn His back on the horror of such destruction, and never again would He strike the world or the living creatures because of man.

And while Noah and his family watched, the world's Maker marked His promise. He threw the colors of heaven through the sky and bent them to the ground like a bow.